PABLO NERUDA
POET OF THE PEOPLE

MONICA BROWN

ILLUSTRATED BY
JULIE PASCHKIS

HENRY HOLT AND COMPANY
NEW YORK

Henry Holt and Company, LLC
Publishers since 1866
175 Fifth Avenue
New York, New York 10010
www.HenryHoltKids.com

Library of Congress Cataloging-in-Publication Data
Brown, Monica.
Pablo Neruda : poet of the people / Monica Brown ; illustrations by Julie Paschkis. — 1st ed.
p. cm.
Includes bibliographical references.
ISBN 978-0-8050-9198-4
1. Neruda, Pablo, 1904–1973—Juvenile literature. 2. Poets, Chilean—20th century—
Biography—Juvenile literature. I. Paschkis, Julie, ill. II. Title.
PQ8097.N4Z593 2011 861.62—dc22 [B] 2010025320

First Edition—2011
Printed in December 2010 in China by South China Printing Co. Ltd.,
Dongguan City, Guangdong Province, on acid-free paper. ∞

1 3 5 7 9 10 8 6 4 2

For Emma, Ollie, Brooke, and Zach
—M. B.

For Joe—my fellow traveler
—J. P.

ONCE there was a little boy named Neftalí,
who loved wild things wildly and quiet things quietly.

From the moment he could talk, Neftalí surrounded himself with words that whirled and swirled, just like the river that ran near his home in Chile.

Neftalí loved to play in the forest, ride horseback,
and swim in the river with his friends.

Neftalí's father was a train conductor, and sometimes
he would take his son with him on the train.

Whenever the train made a stop, Neftalí would run off
into the forest to search for beetles and birds' eggs and tall
ferns that dripped water like tears.

Neftalí wasn't very good at soccer or at throwing acorns like his friends, but he loved to read and discover magic between the pages of books.

A very special teacher named Gabriela Mistral gave him

wonderful books from faraway places, and Neftalí decided

he wanted to be a writer too.

When he was a teenager, Neftalí changed his name to
Pablo Neruda and began publishing his poems. He always
wrote in green ink—the color of the ferns in the forest and
the grass beneath his feet.

Pablo moved to the big city of Santiago and met other writers. Together, Pablo and his friends walked the streets wearing great black capes and tall hats. They talked about books and shared their poems with all who would listen.

Pablo wrote poems about the things he loved—things
made by his artist friends, things found at the marketplace,
and things he saw in nature.

He wrote about scissors and thimbles and chairs and rings.

He wrote about buttons and feathers and shoes and hats.

He wrote about velvet cloth the color of the sea.

Pablo loved opposites, so he wrote about fire and rain and spring and fall.

In the streets and with his friends, Pablo saw joy and
sadness, so he wrote about both.

Pablo loved the stones of Chile.

He wrote about stones rolled by waves onto the beach

and stones polished by sand and salt.

He wrote about stones tumbling down the mountaintops
and stones in the hands of the stonecutters.

Pablo loved the sea and the feel of the sand beneath his feet.

He loved walking along the beach, near his home in Chile.

He found starfish and seaweed, red crabs and green
water. He saw dolphins playing in the surf and rusty anchors
washed ashore.

Pablo wrote about the children who played in the sea foam
and the sand, skipping stones and chasing waves.

He wanted each child to share in Chile's wealth and hope.

Pablo had many homes. One was in Spain, half a world away. This home was called the House of Flowers, because of the red flowers blooming from every corner.

The House of Flowers was always filled with dogs and people young and old.

Because above all things and above all words, Pablo Neruda loved people.

Pablo loved mothers and fathers, poets and artists, children and neighbors, and his many friends around the world. He opened his arms to them all.

When Pablo saw the coal miners working dangerous jobs for little money, he was angry. When he saw that they were cold and hungry and sick, he decided to share their story.

He joined those who fought for justice and wrote poems
to honor all workers who struggled for freedom.

Even when his poems made leaders angry, he would not
be silenced, because he was a poet of the people.

When soldiers came to get him, Pablo hid in the homes of friends and then escaped on a horse over the mountains of Chile.

Pablo Neruda was brave. He wasn't afraid to share the
story of Chile with the world.

Pablo's voice was heard across nations and oceans.

From his poems grew flowers of hope and dreams of peace.

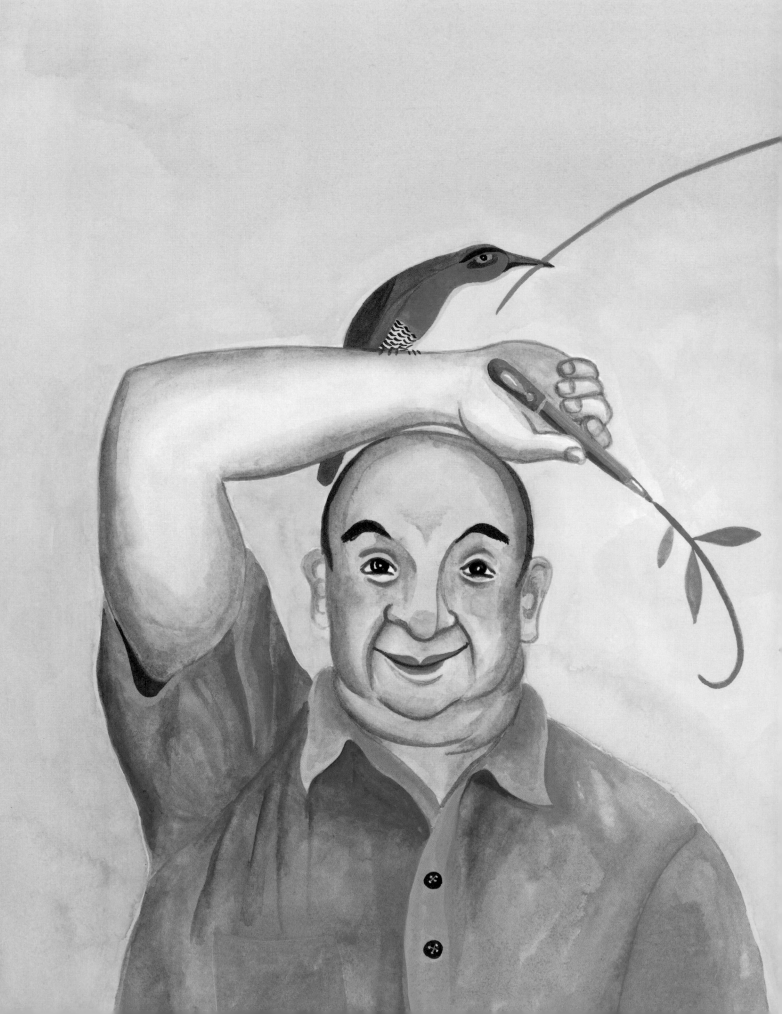

AUTHOR'S NOTE

Pablo Neruda is considered one of the greatest and most influential poets of the twentieth century. He was born Ricardo Eliecer Neftalí Reyes Basoalto in Parral, Chile, in 1904. When Neftalí was growing up, his father didn't approve of his poetry, so Neftalí began publishing poems behind his father's back under the name Pablo Neruda. During his lifetime, Neruda was a student, a diplomat, a senator, an activist, and a fugitive. But always and above all, Pablo Neruda was poet—the poet of the people. Among his most famous works are *Crepusculario*; *Veinte poemas de amor y una canción de desesperada* (*Twenty Love Poems and a Song of Despair*); *España en el corazón* (*Spain in the Heart*); *Canto general*; and *Odas elementales* (*Elementary Odes*). He won the Nobel Prize for Literature in 1971. Pablo Neruda died in Chile in 1973, and a few days later his friend, the poet Yevgeny Yevtushenko, wrote,

> . . . he carries his poetry to the people
> as simply and calmly
> as a loaf of bread.

Today, Pablo's house in Chile, on Isla Negra, still stands. With feelings of love and hope, women and men from all over the world visit to celebrate the poet of the people. Each time we read one of Pablo's poems, he is with us, inspiring us to love and to make our voices heard.

RESOURCES

POETRY BY PABLO NERUDA

Canto General. Translated by Jack Schmitt. Berkeley: University of California Press, 2000.

Elementary Odes. Translated by Carlos Lozano. New York: Gaetano Massa, 1961.

The Heights of Macchu Picchu. Translated by Nathaniel Tarn. New York: Farrar, Straus and Giroux, 1967.

Isla Negra. Translated by Maria Jacketti, Dennis Maloney, and Clark Zlotchew. Buffalo, NY: White Pine Press, 2001.

Odes to Common Things. Translated by Ken Krabbenhoft. Boston: Bulfinch, 1994.

Odes to Opposites. Translated by Ken Krabbenhoft. Boston: Bulfinch, 1995.

Twenty Love Poems and a Song of Despair. Translated by W. S. Merwin. New York: Penguin Books, 2006.

FOR MORE ABOUT NERUDA'S LIFE

Feinstein, Adam. *Pablo Neruda: A Passion for Life.* New York: Bloomsbury, 2004.

Neruda, Pablo. *Memoirs.* Translated by Hardie St. Martin. New York: Farrar, Straus and Giroux, 1977.

See information about Pablo Neruda at the official Nobel Laureate Web site (http://nobelprize.org) and at the Academy of American Poets Web site (www.poets.org).